Best wi

Seeta Kentala

Narayana Smaranams

M.G. Prasad

THOUGHTS TO PONDER
THROUGH THE YEAR

by

M.G. PRASAD

Thoughts to Ponder through the Year

Published by Taranga, New Jersey, USA

No. of pages : x + 366 = 376

Copyright : Author
Revised Edition : August 25, 2014, 1000 copies

ISBN : 978-0-692-26330-3

Printed at : VAGARTHA
149, 8th Cross, N.R. Colony, Bangalore - 560 019, INDIA
Phone : 91-80-22427677, email : vagartha@yahoo.com

Thoughts to Ponder through the Year

I gratefully acknowledge that it is the blessings and grace of my spiritual gurus and yogis-seers, His Holiness Sri Ranga Sadguru and his wife Her Holiness Srimata Vijayalakshmi that have inspired me to offer these "Thoughts to Ponder" I offer these thought-flowers to their Holy feet.

August 25, 2014   M.G. Prasad

ABOUT THIS BOOK

The book, "108 Thoughts to Ponder" first published in December 2000 was very well received by the readers. This reception encouraged me to expand and revise the book to its current form as "Thoughts to Ponder through the Year". I hope this current edition will also be received well.

August 25, 2014
New Jersey, USA.

M.G. Prasad

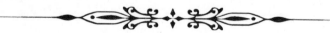

BENEDICTION

With Narayanasmaranas, We raise our hands in benediction over this collection of words of wisdom emanating from a highly cultured person endowed with sweetness and light. The name of the person with his appellation is Dr. M.G. Prasad, for whose well being we are praying.

December 10, 2000   *Sri Sri Rangapriya Sripada Sri Srih*
Bangalore, India

BLESSINGS

This little book written by Dr. M.G. Prasad is big. At the first reading it interests the reader, at the second it guides and at the third it inspires.

December 22, 2000
Bangalore, India

Narayanasmaranas
Swami Paramananda Bharati

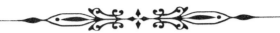

This Publication is in memory of

My parents, M.G. Shakuntala and M.S. Gopalan

and

My father-in-law, N. Ramanuja Iyengar

FOREWORD

When a satellite is launched to reach a predetermined target, it needs directional corrections, due to the various external forces acting on it. Booster Rockets are fired, as and when required, to provide this directional correction and to ensure that the path of travel is always towards the target.

Good books are like Booster Rockets. They correct the attitude of the readers and help them in maintaining a successful, worthy and precious life cycle. Readers' mind, often, get distracted by various negative forces acting, and hence need good books to redirect the mind towards purposeful activities. Every day of the human being should start with a clear vision of the purpose and goal for that day, so that, he could strive and achive worthy results by the time he relaxes in the night.

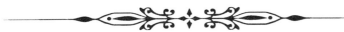

Dr. M.G. Prasad has attempted to assemble and provide the readers with many such efficient booster rockets in his book "Thoughts to ponder throught the Year" This book is an ensemble of 366 thought provoking sayings written by the author, which have been carefully chosen and arranged to ensure that the reader is always directed towards peace, happiness and contentment.

I am sure that this sincere work of Dr. Prasad will find appreciation and encouragement and becomes one of the sought out energy Boosters for the thoughtful readers. Let noble thoughts come to us from all the directions.

August 25, 2014
Bangalore, India.

K.V. Varadaraja Iyengar

ACKNOWLEDGMENTS

I offer my heartfelt gratitude to yogi-seers, His Holiness Sri Sri Rangapriya Sripada Sri Srih and His Holiness Swami Paramananda Bharati for their benediction and blessings.

Thanks to my friend K.V. Varadaraja Iyengar for writing the foreword and also for his suggestions during the revision of this book. Thanks are also due to Ramakrishna Jagadishan and Chetan Bhatt for their suggestions. Thanks are due to Srimati Shamala Iyengar, M.G. Sampath Kumar, Dr. M.G. Narasimhan, N.R. Vijaya Sarathi, M.G. Raghunandan, Mrs. Veena Mohan, Mrs. Manjula Parthasarathy and Mrs. Radhika Srinivas for their support. Also, thanks are due to Dr. Ravi Kulkarni, Dr. S.R. Leela, Mr. G. Yoganarasimha, Mr. Raju Parekh and Mr. Nagaraj Kowshik for their help. I thank Geetha Prasad, Teju Prasad, Raju Prasad and Lindsey Hack for their help and support. Thanks to Vagartha for its excellent production of this book.

M.G. Prasad

January 1

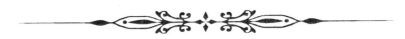

The privileges of a human being
are - to wonder, to ponder, to
practice and realize.

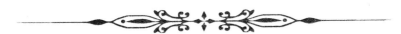

Learning is the birth right of a
human being.

January 3

Basically, there are two kinds of knowledge; they are knowledge of the things observed and knowledge of the observer.

January 4

True knowledge always wins.

It is the motive that determines
the value of an action.

God has to be realized in oneself, by oneself, for oneself but with the grace and guidance of a Guru who has realized God.

At the least, one can only
purify oneself.

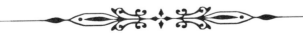

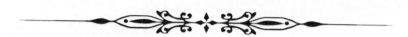

There is no competition
in God-realization.

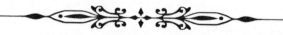

Never quit the question until question itself quits.

For every question that rises
within oneself, one has the ability
to seek and find its answer.

If you are right, never quit.

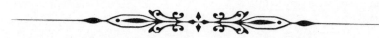

Practice is harder than
beginning a good habit.

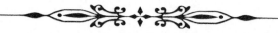

It is only spiritual relationship
that survives the test of time.

Seeking with faith results
in seeing.

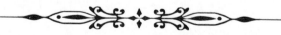

In spiritual pursuit, one is either a seeker or a seer.

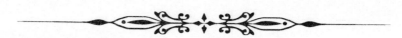

Prayer is an action with an attitude of gratitude to God.

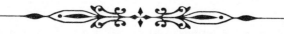

Look for the cause of
your problems
independent of where it is.

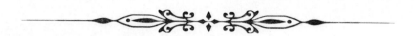

God-realization
is surely possible as God
is not bound by time and space.

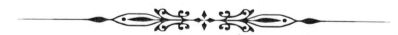

We seem to spend more effort on acquiring things that we do not carry with us when we die, than on things which we carry.

Purity of heart and
clarity of mind are
essential for a joyful life.

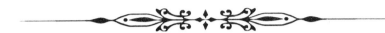

The more one knows about life,
the less aggressive will one be.

January 22

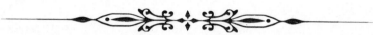

There are a few that are always at peace and remaining ones are happy and unhappy at different times. But there is no one who is unhappy all the time.

Ability to change the course of
life is a characteristic that
separates human beings
from others.

Learning has a beginning
but no end; whereas ignorance
has no beginning but an end.

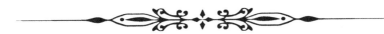

Learning a subject to teach
makes one to learn better.

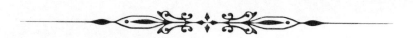

The true Personality of a person
is shown by what the person
really thinks of others.

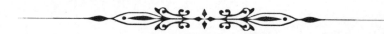

That which is inevitable
can only be understood.

The real human values do not change; it is only the ways we regard these values that change.

The more one understands one's limitations, the more one understands one's freedom.

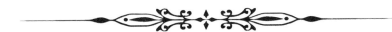

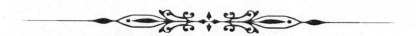

As one can only speak of part of the whole, it is wiser to attempt to see the whole.

In the short run, perception can be stronger than fact, but in the long run fact survives.

February 1

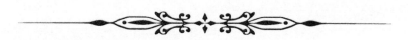

It is the unison in thought,
speech and action that great
people strive for in life.

The shorter the speech,
the longer it takes to prepare.

The quality of a work
is in its details.

February 4

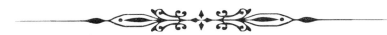

Intelligence results in harmony
rather than conflict between
short and long term goals.

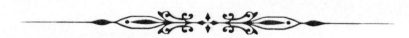

Lack of knowledge is the cause of misery.

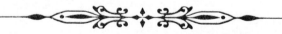

February 6

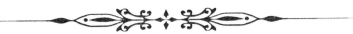

Connection with Eternity
leads to God-realization.

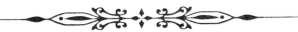

Only truth can break
the chain of lies.

Often 'greed' comes in the
disguise of a 'need.'

February 9

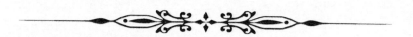

It is more difficult to control one's own mind than to control someone else's mind.

One loses when one gives up
fighting a bad habit.

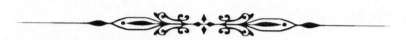

There is no moment of time
when we cannot learn
from nature.

Human mind is the most
powerful thing because it is
the gift from God.

Transformation of a caterpillar to a butterfly is God's way of showing humans that it is possible to transform from materialistic to spiritual level.

G.O.D. is an acronym for the entity that governs the cycle of Generation, Operation and Dissolution. Everything except GOD goes through this cycle.

A value is like the fixed end of a measuring tape that can be used to measure things in one's life.

One's freedom seems to be
limited by one's own fate.

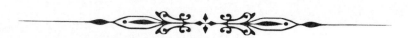

Spiritual pursuit can be seen as
efforts of realizing the relationship
between one's own freewill
and God's will.

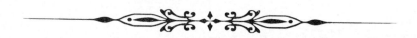

Everything begins with love,
even hate begins with love.

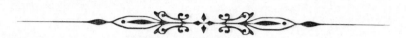

Learning is a continuous feedback process of going from the known to the unknown.

A hungry mind, if not fed with
the food of noble thoughts, will
find its own food, usually junk.

We usually ignore our enemies
within us who hurt us more than
enemies outside.

Knowledge and Action
can be seen as
two legs of a human being.

It is useful when knowledge manifests in action and action further deepens the knowledge.

One can justify one's mistake
but cannot cheat oneself.

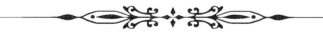

February 25

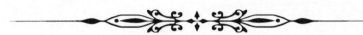

Truth is stronger than a lie
because a lie operates in
the disguise of truth.

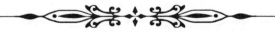

Past, present and future are inter-related. One needs to understand one's past to improve one's future through present actions.

Although thinking does not cost anything, it is still the most difficult thing to do.

It is not how much one reads,
writes or speaks that matters
but what really matters is
how deeply one ponders.

Desire motivates everyone.

March 1

Pondering over a sublime and
spiritually elevating subject
can control a wandering mind.

Patience is
not giving up the right path.

Everyone is equally eligible
to develop spiritual insight.

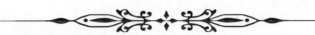

It is the same mind
that is used to either
think or to worry.

March 5

Seeking leads to truth.

March 6

Comparison
is an essential part of life.

It is only when we interact
with the truly great ones,
our thinking changes.

Attentive listening
requires the control of mind.

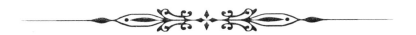

It is a fact that no child at birth
expresses jealousy, hatred and
violence. They are acquired later.

March 10

At birth, no child is attached to any physical thing but at death, every person will be detached from all physical things.

March 11

Mind seems to travel
faster than light.

In spite of great technological
developments, control of mind,
still, seems to be the
most difficult task.

Science and Spirituality
are essential tools
to understand life.

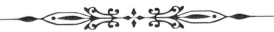

It is the interactions between
the components that
characterize the system.

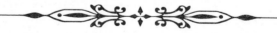

One should not forget to ponder
on birth and death although
living occurs between them.

In dance, music controls the
movements.

March 17

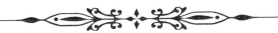

As one can go after
whatever one desires,
it is important to decide
on what to desire.

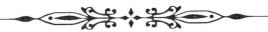

Our spirituality shows up in
our internal and external
responses to others.

Understanding speech requires
intelligence. Enjoying music
requires feelings.

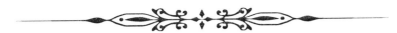

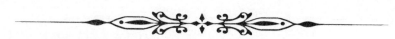

Interaction with others only at physical and mental levels without the spiritual level usually results in conflict.

One should learn more about
oneself by getting into
other's shoes.

Faulty assumptions usually lead to erroneous judgments.

Keeping an open mind is
essential in learning.

Fame should follow a person,
but not the other way round.

One should constantly assess
the state of mind within.

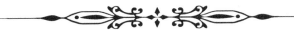

Mind will be free as long as it
dwells truly in the abode of
freedom called God.

March 27

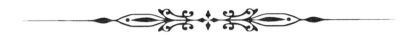

It is the audio-visual input to the
mind that matters in spiritual
development.

Usually for a thing to cook it has
to be boiled. Only simmering
will not cook.

The great ones do not
compromise on the
quality of their work.

One develops a deeper thinking
ability as one takes full
responsibility for one's actions
and reactions.

Jealousy obstructs one's own
spiritual growth.

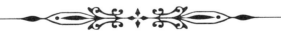

Internalization of great values
results in spiritual insight.

One needs to begin with
oneself to understand others.

April 3

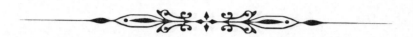

Mind is the most powerful tool.
It should be kept clean and sharp
to achieve great things.

Reflective thinking uniquely
characterizes a human being.
Hence, deeper the better.

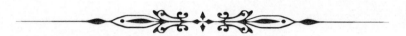

Let the mind wander to ponder
over everlasting values.

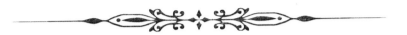

When one masters the alphabets
of life, the literature of life
can be studied.

April 7

Each traveler is alone, but the journey is together.

A person becomes well rounded
based on the deep studies of
great lives and great writings.

April 9

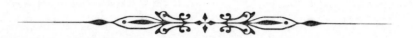

It is always a challenge to bring the mind to the present, because the mind always escapes to dwell on either the past or the future.

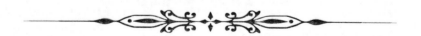

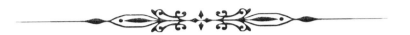

If scientific and technological developments are attributed to human ability, to whom can the abilities of humans be attributed ?

April 11

The only way to avoid fear of
loneliness is to realize the
companionship of the ever-present
and all-pervading God.

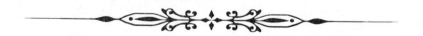

April 12

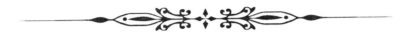

There is always a difference between
what we think of ourselves and what
others think of us; so it matters how
we react to the difference.

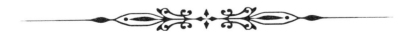

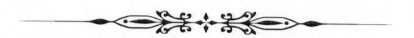

We feel happy when we freely praise the truly noble qualities of others, but we feel unhappy when we are forced to praise others.

As one needs a clear mirror to
observe oneself physically so also
one needs a self-realized soul as
Guru to realize oneself.

The most difficult challenge for
anyone is to honestly deal
face-to-face with oneself.

One's disappointments are
based on one's expectations.

The mystery of human life
is in its ability
to make a choice.

One needs to check one's ego
on a daily basis.

Failure provides
an opportunity for
self-evaluation.

A mission without vision
is like moving
in a path without a goal.

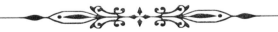

Every thought and action together
needs to produce a light as in the
case of a match stick rubbing
the paper.

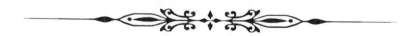

April 22

Every sound carries Information.

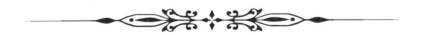

Any assumption about a human
being can go wrong because of
the human free will.

It is a spiritual struggle to
tune our free-will to be in
harmony with God's will.

Any Job, well-done, is the result of God's grace and human effort.

April 26

Anger can help if it is directed towards one's own deficiencies.

One needs to be strict when
dealing with oneself but
moderate with others.

When mind is focused
on a moving goal
it experiences stress.

It is better and safer to
ask than to assume.

A joyful life is the result of
keeping mind simple and pure.

It does not matter which
compartment in a train one sits
as long as it is connected
to the engine.

May 2

Psychology deals with the analysis of mind and spirituality deals with the source of mind.

Roots of a tree
govern its fruits.

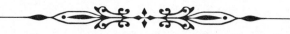

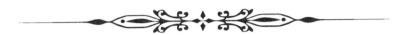

It is a mystery that the infinite
comes out of finite. For example
infinite number of waves
from the ocean.

It is through devotion
that an action results
in deeper knowledge.

For harmony in one's life a
balance between individual
and universal values
needs to be achieved.

As a circle of smaller radius
can be drawn within another
circle with a larger radius,
so also local thinking is to be
made a part of global thinking.

May 8

One should always look at the
waves as part of the ocean.

First think before you speak or act, then think after you speak or act; this will help keep your wisdom intact.

May 10

The Communication gaps begin
within oneself between one's own
thoughts and actions.

May 11

One's fate seems to be the
result of exercising of one's
freedom in the past.

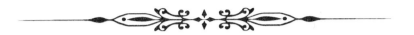

To decide is an individual act.
However, this act is a result of
interaction with others.

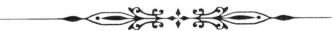

Nature seems to deny the
death to be its final event.

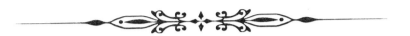

It is all in the way one looks at things. A point is a circle of zero radius. A straight line is a circle with radius equal to infinity.

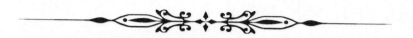

The human life is an opportunity
given to realize the secrets
of birth and death.

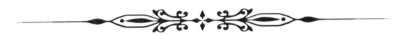

The phrase 'Life goes on' means
that death does not stop the
movement of life.

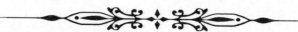

A finite string with fixed boundary conditions has infinite modes of vibrations. This means that life between physical birth and death experiences in infinite modes.

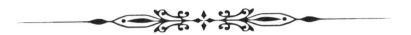

One should make an effort, daily,
to increase one's freedom
to dwell on universal and
eternal aspects.

Slavery to gain knowledge
is better than
slavery to gain money.

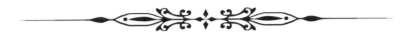

Whatever depends on time and space is not permanent.

We have time to worry
but not to think.

Discrimination in desire
is wisdom.

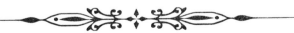

Life denies
death.

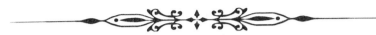

Death gives
Importance to life.

The jouney of life is a
continuous effort in going
from known to unknown.

For a play performed on stage
the director is God, but in life,
God is the director.

There are two kinds of desires;
the first kind needs more
and more money, the second
kind needs more and more freedom.

It is a gift that humans have, the ability to control their urges.

What really matters in life is how much one knows about oneself rather than how many other things one knows.

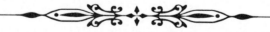

Life and death seem to laugh at
each other's victory.

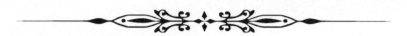

Gratitude is a spiritual quality.

It is the desire to own a materialistic thing that has the seed of misery.

June 2

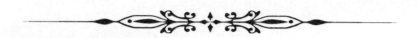

Contentment is a conscious
decision to eliminate one's greed.

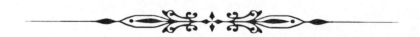

154

Desirable desire has to win over
undesirable desire.

One needs to make intentional
effort to forget unpleasant
experience.

June 5

Look for a pleasant future and
overlook the unpleasant past.

Keep a company that leads to
spiritual growth.

Never give up humility.

June 8

Be like the spring season that
brings flowers of joy for others.

Let the spiritual vision
govern your life.

Never compromise quality
over quantity.

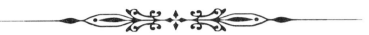

Make remembrance of God
as the thread passing through
all daily activities.

Learn from anyone, anywhere.

Do not make age a barrier to
learn from a person.

Never allow
inferiority or superiority complex
into your personality.

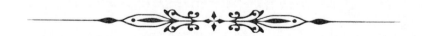

Do not let vocabulary confuse
with the contents in a
person's speech.

Challenge yourself
and
Improve.

Do not be indifferent to make efforts to know what happens after death during lifetime.

One can only repent and change
before death.

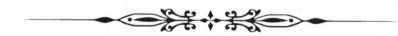

Be brief in speaking but not
in thinking.

Never engage or continue in the
company that weakens you
spiritually or intellectually.

June 21

Never allow intellectual blindness
to occur due to non-reading of
works of great authors.

Travel to learn and
learn to travel.

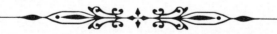

Remember that death can
call upon anyone at anytime
and anywhere.

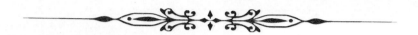

Never forget that the potential to succeed is within oneself.

Being jealous at another person's success is a step towards failure in spiritual development.

Look at nature for reference in judging human values.

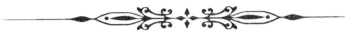

It is extraordinary to love
without being loved.

Visit holy places to absorb
spiritual energy.

Inner eyes can see
what external eyes cannot see.

Past cannot be fully understood
and future cannot be fully
predicted.

July 1

Although short-term goals are important in life, long-term goals define the life.

Life becomes meaningful
when the full meaning
of life is realized.

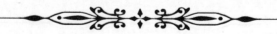

Is life cyclical or linear?

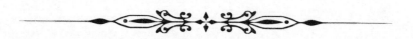

It is a desire driven life, so it is desires that determines our life.

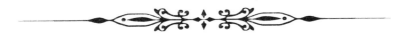

It is through the connection with
the spiritually realized ones that
we become really spiritual.

Detachment should be
the result of wisdom
to annihilate the desire.

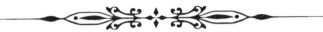

Advancement in spiritual
development requires serious
efforts.

July 8

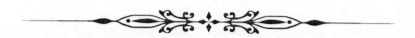

One should never ignore to learn
from one's mistakes.

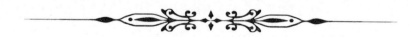

We become spiritually rich
as we keep an account of
our thoughts, like money.

Mental laziness
is more detrimental than
physical laziness.

Sincere and in-depth efforts are essential to succeed.

One should see oneself,
spiritually, in others.

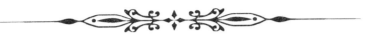

An inquiring mind
keeps one young.

It is the inner personality that
reflects a person.

July 15

You are never alone.

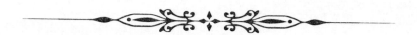

Spiritual solutions should not be ruled out in any situation.

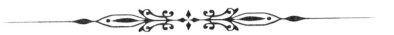

Focus on the changeless when
dealing with changes.

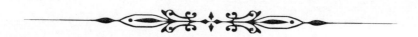

Vision should guide the mission.

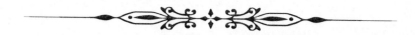

Different foods and tastes
indicate diversity;
Hunger indicates unity.

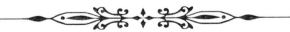

Rethinking deepens
understanding of oneself.

Gratitude is a spiritual quality.

It is not possible to have complete
control of body. It is not easy to
have complete control of mind.

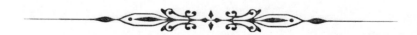

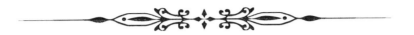

How much we truly understand
ourselves is more important than
how much others understand us.

As moving things are recognized in
relation to a non-moving reference,
so we need to search for the
non-moving reference to understand
our wandering mind.

July 25

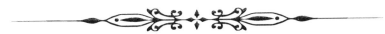

It is only by reading the
literature that has stood the test
of time that we can expand
our mind into eternity.

Our spiritual advancement
depends on the extent of our
spiritual effort in our
wakeful state.

In reviewing things of our past,
the less we feel that we should
have done things differently the
more we have made progress.

It is much easier to deal with a
person with ignorance than a
person with indifference.

A message of a tree is that one
needs to grow from physical earth
into spiritual space.

Truth stands
by its own strength.

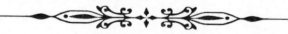

True knowledge cannot
feed Ego.

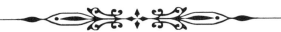

Conflict between two people is conflict between two levels of knowledge.

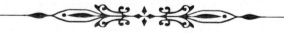

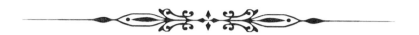

Internal beauty is more beautiful
than external beauty.

August 3

The mystery of the inability to precisely predict human behavior is a clue to understanding life.

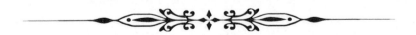

The perceived nature is
much easier to understand
than true human nature.

The mystery of speech is in its bridging thought and action.

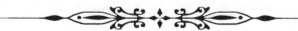

Keeping the word will make
the person live longer than
physical life.

Let the words from the mouth
bring what is in the head
through the heart.

Light is only a witness
to our interaction with objects.

Sound is a form of light.

August 10

Yoga is the way to happiness
through happiness but one need
to work hard for it.

August 11

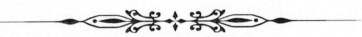

If things are going easy then
look out for the direction
it is going.

August 12

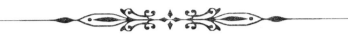

Although where one is born is
important, it is much
more important to find
why one is born.

We need to thank God for giving us an opportunity to learn from animals and nature and for using that learning to become divine.

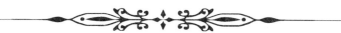

Mind is like a transparent glass.
Only when it is totally clean,
will the spiritual vision
be possible.

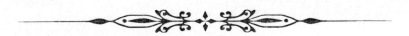

Education based values should
form the values of life.

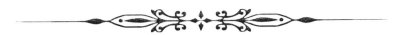

Never give up introspection.

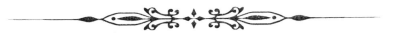

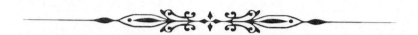

Development of detachment to transient things leads to spiritual development.

If you do not harness the fire within, with the help of a kind-hearted Guru, then the same fire will burn you.

It is only God that can be
seen in everything.

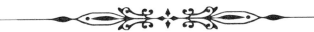

A great person is
one who has realized the
greatest thing namely God.

August 21

It seems that God will evaluate only how we use our free will in our thought, speech and actions.

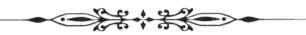

When one continues to wonder
and ponder about the marvels
of nature then one gets a
child-like mind that can see God.

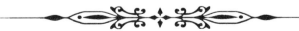

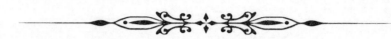

Spiritual values should
not be ignored in favor of
worldly values.

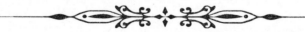

It is very important to keep a
close watch on desires that
drive one's life.

Never assume anything
and do not doubt everything.

Everyone is driven by self-interest
but the understanding of self
varies from person to person.

Short cuts should
not result in negative
long terms effects.

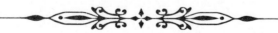

It is easier to change yourself
than to change others.

To lie is to intentionally allow
a communication gap between
one's thought and speech.

As waves and ocean are inseparable, so also the manifestation of life and God are inseparable.

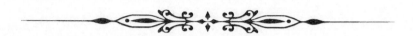

As a thread connects all flowers
in a garland,
God connects all our activities.

Truth is a bridge that takes one from illusion back to reality.

September 2

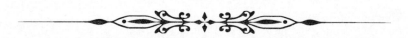

The nature of our effort should
be vectorial which means both
the magnitude and direction
of effort are important.

Pure mind is light and
impure mind is heavy.

A true scientific attitude
results in an open mind.

September 5

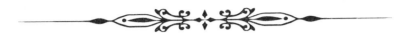

We should not allow our outer
eyes to blind the inner eye.

As one grows older, one needs
to introspect the relationship
between oneself and the body
and how it has changed
since childhood.

True great people achieve
greatness through their vision
and actions of universal
relevance.

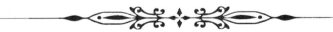

Learning and teaching are
concurrent activities
for the growth of knowledge.

A true scholar is
free from jealousy.

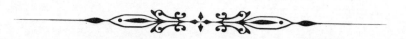

The speech, not backed up
by sincerity, is like the sound
of an empty vessel.

Never confuse external
expression for internal
understanding.

Spiritual equality is a fact.

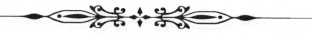

It is in details that clarity
comes through.

September 14

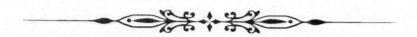

Today connects yesterday
and tomorrow.

September 15

Today is an opportunity to
learn from yesterday's lessons
and work towards a
better tomorrow.

Future is more important than
the past as one can visualize it
and put efforts to achieve it.

Action and direction need to be in harmony in achieving a goal.

Learn to smile as a child
because it is natural.

September 19

Nature is teaching all the time, it is up to us to learn from it.

We need to look within, as it
is the only hope for finding
the solution.

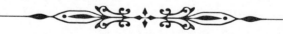

The forces are invisible so we
need insight to deal with them.

Self-transformation is essential
before attempting to
transform others.

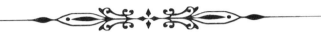

Wisdom brings
Contentment.

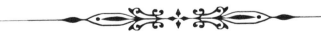

Time management refers to
managing ourselves within the
laws of time.

Money cannot buy values.

To be happy in life, we need
to earn things that money
cannot buy.

What is invisible in a person
can be more important
than the visible.

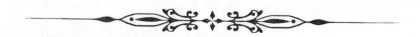

You make a scholar happy when
you respect scholarship.

A narrow-minded person would
be unable to understand a
broad-minded person.

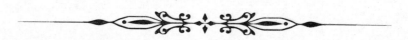

Spend time in the company
of truly great people.

October 1

Sincerity lies in not
compromising oneself till
one achieves excellence.

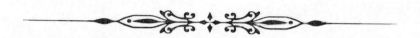

If one is not free from jealousy
then one will be neither happy
nor make spiritual progress.

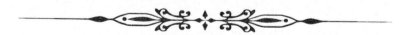

The journey of mind inwards
makes life spiritual; where as its
journey outwards makes it
materialistic.

As we water the roots to obtain good fruits, we need to nurture values to lead a good life.

October 5

It is hard to put the train
the first time on tracks.

If there are no values in life,
then what is the value of
that life?

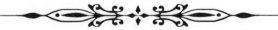

October 7

The habit of telling lie leads
one not to believe in truth.

The true equality is that everyone can realize GOD.

A life without goal has no
sense of achievement.

Nature is an
important teacher.

Mind is purified by
spiritual practices.

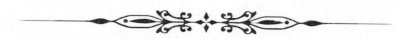

The common thing between
circles of different
radii is 360 degrees.

Generally any achievement brings with it an ego, but it is upto the individual not to be influenced by it.

Broad mindedness
brings more friends.

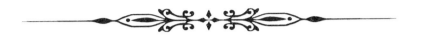

Nature changes as per the
will of the non-changing God.

Nurturing the roots
will yield good fruits.

October 17

The cycles of nature teach
us fixed laws.

Time is moving continuously
but experiences seem
to be discrete.

In a movie, pictures move on a non-moving screen, similarly moving things have a non-moving reference.

A lie can never defy truth.

October 21

One needs to try to know
everything possible about
something specific in life.

If one listens with an intention
to learn and teach, then
one listens better.

If one can change oneself,
then one may be able to
change others.

The law of karma says that everyone is responsible for their own circumstances.

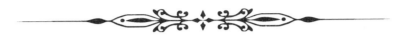

Sometimes, it is harder to
control reaction than action.

Comparing oneself with others
may be unavoidable,
but how one uses that in life
makes the difference.

A purposeful life has
core values.

Past memories
drive the future.

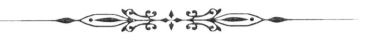

It takes effort to remember
those from whom we have
received favors.

The spiritual development
depends on the food
for thoughts.

October 31

The childhood, youth and
old age are the
expressions of time.

One needs to see nature
for Inspiration.

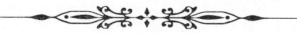

One needs to question oneself.

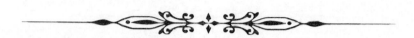

One needs to analyze thought,
speech and action.

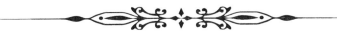

Time is impartial and an
independent observer
of human events.

Learn from the past
for a better future.

God speaks through nature.

One's perception of time
changes with time.

November 8

Human life is characterized by creativity.

313

If developments in science
and technology have not enhanced
human values, then what is the
use of these developments?

The spiritual development depends on the extent to which one realises oneself.

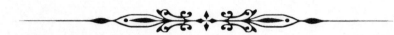

Creating a bad habit is much easier than breaking it.

Comparison with others
can disrupt one's contentment.

Like an agriculturist one should cultivate noble thoughts in the landscape of one's mind.

If mind is not kept elevated
by effort, then it will find its
way down.

Insight is developed through inward journey of mind.

Future can induce fear, but hope and experience provide strength to deal with it.

One should be truthful in speech
as it is the bridge between
one's thoughts and actions.

Never quit Learning.

The great ones make no
difference between their speech
and actions.

Is free-will really free?

Practice and patience are
essential to achieve a goal.

Intelligence should reflect
in quality of one's life.

The advantage of telling truth
over a lie is that one need
not remember.

Success without struggle
seems impossible

There are more things that pull
our mind down than those
that uplift our mind.

Solitude and spiritual
practice go together.

Human beings have the
advantage of learning
from everything.

Abilities of learning
and
teaching co-exist in everyone.

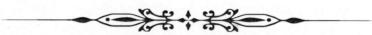

One should try to justify
oneself with true references
rather than by oneself.

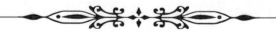

Although there is a choice for
thinking either before or after
an action, the intelligent one
chooses the first one.

December 1

Although future is based on
past and present, it is still
unpredictable.

December 2

The journey to seek truth starts with faith and ends in true experience.

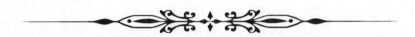

Is time continuous or discrete?

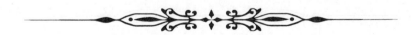

Ego is very powerful because
it can stop one's growth.

A teacher always learns and
one who continuously learns
can only teach.

A teacher is one who removes
the obstacles to learning.

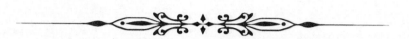

Listening to and telling
truth needs courage.

December 8

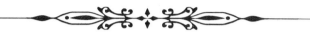

Spiritual development is a
result of keeping inner fire
burning.

One can take the mind as deep
as one practices silence.

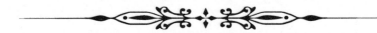

December 10

Mind wanders by nature.
It is only by linking it to
God that one can tame it.

One should develop the
ability to keep the mind
free at one's will.

December 12

One should gain objective
knowledge through ones
experiences.

December 13

Concurrency in one's Thought,
Speech and Action
makes one great.

Free will and fate
are interdependent
in one's life.

December 15

What survives when a person
dies is what people remember.

The real victory is the
victory over death.

As soon as one is born,
death becomes a companion.

December 18

God is a sure companion who
stays till the end.

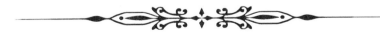

Time that does not yield
knowledge
is a wasted time.

One should convert information
to knowledge through
intelligence.

There are two types of desires namely desirable desires and undesirable desires. Ultimately both are undesirable.

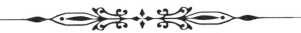

Deep thinking and shallow
thinking are two ends
of human mind.

Self-evaluation is more
important than evaluation
of others.

It is through the language
of soul that one
understands life.

Real silence is the
silence of mind.

It is important to know that one
needs different foods for body,
intellect and spirit.

Freedom of spirit is more
important than
freedom of body.

One needs to achieve self-control
through internal strength not by
external suppression.

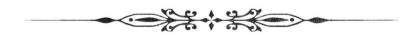

One needs to guard against
any action before it becomes
a habit.

December 30

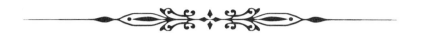

Spiritual practices feed the spirit.

In summary, understanding
begins with oneself and
ends in realizing the self.

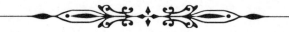